DEFINING ATLAS

STONE MICHAELS

Defining Atlas

ISBN:	Paperback:	978-1-63945-071-8
	Ebook:	978-1-63945-072-5

Writers' Branding1800-608-6550
www.writersbranding.com
orders@writersbranding.com

Contents

Like the demigod from which it takes its name, *Defining Atlas* is a durable, uplifting volume. A strong current of self-affirmation, self-love, and self- confidence runs through this work, and readers will come away feeling their spirits improved.
Sturdy, exuberant verse.

-The Kirkus Review

Stone Michaels's *Defining Atlas* contains poems that illuminate both the poet himself and the God he gives all glory to. In plainspoken language, Michaels praises God while exploring the everyday heartache we all endure. The result is a collection that many will find inspiring through its prayerful self- examination.
Defining Atlas brings together poems that look both upward toward heaven and at the earth beneath our feet. Within the collection, Michaels seems to shoulder the weight of his own burdens while seeking to show others a path that will lead to paradise.

-The Clarion Review

In his debut book of poetry, Michaels captures the various characteristics of life. He tantalizes his readers with the human condition, which is consistently challenged by its spirituality. His colorful collection passes through the heart and soul of our darkest and brightest moments of our journey through life. Exiting with a graceful bow and standing ovation,
Michaels projects a thriving vision and striving purpose that we are defining and refining ourselves while enduring like the great Greek Titan Atlas, who's symbolized with a timeless image of a man carrying the world on his back. And like that Titan, we carry a certain poise and tenacity of the brunt of a forever-changing world. In his works, he shows us that strength, heartache, love, courage, and most importantly sincerity, play an intimate experience to our destiny.

From a southern-raised adolescent to a military veteran to corporate America, Michaels believes that you should never be a victim of your circumstances but a victim of God's success! Like Atlas, it takes endurance to live life. He presses and challenges us to be more than our present. Growing up in a family comprised of ministers, veterans, nurses, and educators, he absorbs the combination of hard work and spiritual humility. His lasting impression that he would like to leave for future generations is simply to encourage a despaired heart.

The Humble Prayer of the Preacher's Son

Here I am with a bowed head and a humbled heart
I continue, like Job, pressing toward the mark
I'm but a servant with unwanted iniquities
With hope in my heart sprinkled with loyalty You see,
I try day in and day out . . .
Trying to be like the others
Making people shout
Letting them know You're near
Letting them know You can hear
The testimony of the heart is all I have left
With the capacity of a long-suffering soul praying for help
I know that love is always the key
Even though sometimes it's not free
So please keep me in Your grace
As I reach out and continue to embrace
The path before me . . . I know I will stray
But I'll always pray . . . humbly, I say
Thank you for truly understanding my spiritual forte
As I close my prayer with a comforting smile,
I'm always glad we talked for a while

The Heart that Could

Time has shown me the thoroughness of Love
Forever exposed to the bludgeoning cause by his dear brother, Life
Nothing can compare his never ending strife
The longing and entrusted duties of humanity for us to prove
Things that happen for a reason is our heart of hearts spiritual ground;
Believing as if we're on the A-train upward-bound
But we're too practical and logical down here in the flesh
Here where Pain and Life are kind of . . . you know . . . meshed
Here where the heart is our biggest duality of our all and all
Fused with our minds and souls . . . Oh, we do try!
To separate them all if they don't play, lay, or stay together but . . .
The heart that could—ha! —the heart that would . . . .
The heart that stood through it all . . . it keeps going.
Through it all, it heals and wills keeping us infatuated.
I will forever let the heart know—if it hasn't taught me anything—
thanks for letting me know
If I died today as dancing with Life on a stage and closing before I go;
Thank you, Heart, for orchestrating the show!

Windowlizing

They say the eyes are windows to the soul . . .
Something that's worth the hold
The long pause that makes us reminisce
Watching life entertain us in a frisk
Staring out wondering about days
Examining the how and why about this maze
Yeah, I'm just here . . . me and the window
Watching life go from zero to hero
I stare out into whatever that could be forever
Looking around here and wondering about earth and heaven
Thinking my world had slipped . . . mmm . . . never
Taking in all my emotions that could be
All of the "what ifs" and "possible maybes"
And the "don'ts" and "discouraging wants . . ."
Embracing the need to believe,
The longing to heal,
Getting rid of the status quo . . .
Just to live inspirationally into tomorrow

The Intimacy (InToMeSheSee)

She sees a shattered heart
One that beats apart . . .
Still not broken from the start
The one that beats with remarks
She sees my past and future all at once
The love she knew that flaunts
She sees it all and still has a rush
The intimacy . . . mmm . . . what a rush!
. . . and still she'd blush

Raindrops

Well, well, I think I see the sky
Dull and gray
Its explicit looks of dye
Colors of mystic overlapping, fading, and fading away
Life and death . . . They seem rolled up in one
The dull sky stretches across the earth farther than
the sound of the great thunder
The raindrops fell as if the clouds gave birth.
It poured like tears
Drop by drop, symbolizing every emotion
Flowing wild and free like an experienced deer
Relaxing and pleasant, it seems by its drowsy motion
And it poured . . .
And poured with Life it came
And *drip drop* . . . *drip drop* . . . beautiful rain!

Ambition

My time is well spent on many things . . .
But Life is what it brings
This is Ambition
It is the juice that spins
In eternal time flowing in my mind,
In my soul intertwine things that can't be defined;
Divine . . . that is the very pulse of my total existence
The very being of my soul and heart that makes it all worth it
What I am and what I do are not for everybody
But the results of everything I do is for the world
Who am I? I am the matter, the vessel of my father
The mouthpiece of a life well spent in denial until I saw the light
The true light that always shined in darkness
Because only then the brightest of the reflection of its rays will be seen before man
And here I stand . . . Ambition
The thing that pumps in the back of my soul
It comes out no matter how old . . . Ambition
Who? . . . And then and now and forever
. . . Ambition

Wake Up!

When the sun comes and welcomes dawn, Wake up!
There's something good here for you
Your purpose can never be defined by just one blue
Your destiny awaits you
You are the apple of His eye
He restores and gives us a new blessing every sunrise
Wake up! Face and take your day
You are the essential piece of the way
Wake up! Because without you, hopes and dreams and possibilities and purpose will just lay
So wake up! And see the tomorrow, and honor the ones who could not stay
Now their history and future lie with you
Remember, your purpose can never be defined by just one blue
So . . . Wake up! Wake up!

The Retro

Being in the retrospect
Revealing truth
How God moves us like a big smile from ear to ear
Our experiences that carve out our future past
Not prone to one state because like the Retro, it'll change and won't last
It's a glimpse of our prophetic wisdom leaning forward into the betterment of ourselves
We choose to shun away from it because we are comfortable wearing veils
I pray every day for the latter of our selfishness, choosing not to be in tune
Not acknowledging the Retro is truly being blind to the fact
Seeing and understanding the glimpses of God's plan for you . . . mmm
. . . How about that!

Invincible

I am bigger than out!
Don't make a mark on my grave When I come about,
Don't worry! I'll pave.
I am a dreamer, seeing the way beyond what's here
I am a dream chaser without fear
The sounds of victory announce my presence ... pitched perfectly clear
The disturbance of life trying to interrupt will cost tears
That's just a small price to pay
For a chance for a vision to become the only way
Invincibility will not let me give into the settlement of life
Even though I've tried to keep it at bay
It pours out of me in every breath and stride I take
Living it and doing it despite the noise it makes
Being Invincible ... through wisdom and just standing
Being Invincible ... through just the idea of flying without landing
Give thanks to the past that taught
And the future mistakes it caught
I'm still here ... just me, just to be
Another chapter of a glorious history
Not dreading a sunrise
Because I don't fret time
Knowing what's truly for me is mine

For now, I just have to be patient and let it come into focus for me
I'm talking about that overflow of abundance that only comes through that Invincibility
Withstanding life and cherishing every and anything that could be
Not forgetting the vulnerability
I stay how I am without denial
Even doing a pride check for those selfless miles
Absorb it all . . . That's how it'll stay and I pray . . . Invincible . . .

The Mississippi I Knew ... Home

Well, here I am ... back in the homeland
Where the grass is green like no other (pretty much year-round)
A place where hospitality is the crown
It's summertime, hanging out with my old used-to-be-mean,
didn't- pay-me- any-attention, sometimes-fake but great friends
It's different but the same ... tucked neatly into its old frame
Well, the Mississippi I knew
Where summertime was filled with melons to eat
A place where everyone grew
Great food that—mmm! —how the treats were so sweet!
Where morals couldn't be beat
Where everyone knew your family or kin
We all stuck together through thick or thin ...
The Mississippi I knew, where we shared laughter and pain equally the same,
Where we shared our life's burdens throughout the week
And fellowship was the key on Sunday's and Wednesday's church meets
Where the women were beautiful and of all shapes and sizes
They carried themselves like queens rising
The men were hardworkers, and of course, they were kings too
Filled with southern pride from their stroll to everything they do
Well, the Mississippi I knew

Where summertime was filled with melons to eat
A place where everyone grew
Great food that—mmm! —how the treats were so sweet!
Where morals couldn't be beat
Where everyone knew your family or kin
We all stuck together, of course, through thick or thin . . . Home.

’Til Days End

’Til the sky falls, I’m forever embracing your smile
’Til the sun turns, my heart will always burn
’Til the Angels come, you and I are a sum
’Til the days of glory, I’ll continue to try to fly
’Til my thoughts cease, I will always believe
’Til the earth tumbles, my soul will stay humble
’Til the sun sets, I will never forget
’Til the earth stops, my heart will not
’Til days end, beyond infinity, I’ll defend
’Til Tomorrow greets me with a “Begin!”
’Til days end, again

My Breakthrough Walls

I slipped and fell into inevitable
The expectations of the things that surrounded me would be my biggest sin
I was not true from within
Now I've tapped the longing of my thirst
It's also the cure to my surrounding curse
They stood as a dominance, a thinking-all-knowing force
Knowing my very existence but not my source
And then it happened only when I begin to climb
Finally, resolution to be victorious would be mine It was just as real as my imagination . . .
And then I awoke, realizing the walls were temporary boundaries for my situation
And so I grew and . . . I broke . . . no more the victim;
I became stronger
The walls were indeed no longer

My Love, Not Back

She was the reason for all the seasons
She wasn't my God but merely a gift
I loved her with all my feelings
She had a drive with a shift
My Love with no way back
My love was strong . . . what a catch!
She was everything but not my match
My love, not back
One day I thought she will return
With a warm heart claiming she was wrong
I would welcome her with loving arms
Back to a place where I thought she'll belong
And I still was left . . . My love, my love
My love . . . not back
I've carried a heavy heart through it all
Pressing through, stumbling, and falling
This was inevitable and quite all right
Because the victory was not in my fight,
And I still was left . . . My love, my love
My love . . . not back
As enchanting as it may seem
Oh, how I wish Life was more to me
Filled with love and precious dreams!
But this is reality; we crave Life's esteem
And I left her chasing a dream
My destiny was wilderness,
And my strength was not in my withdrawal
But understanding how Love was for all
My love, my love
My love . . . not back

From the ashes . . . I am

I am victory in its rawest form
I am hope that never conform
I am the will, the drive, and the truth
I am like everyone, like you
The seed-bloomed opportunity
Displaying my ambition at best
Silent success could be my rest
Pledged by the blood-given immunity
From being torn . . . I am
Burnt ashes . . . redemption . . .I am a champion
I was born to be second, third, fourth . . . that's me
Chances I have . . . I am
From the desperation to aspirations
From the ashes . . . I am

Forever January

Long days and nights of mysteries
With no irony or iniquities
Forever fallen from the hearts of all
Forever fallen from a cause
Strange lands of deserted times
The secrets to life, I wish they were mine
Satisfied with enough Ways paved but scuffed
Forever I stay in the rain
Wishing for that eternal pain
For it's easier to accept
Than to live life with regret
History was right about one thing
Man's love and hate it brings
A torn-but-forever-seen existence
He stands next to me with constant consistence
January, my long and thoughtful host
Let us both acquire a toast
To the heavens we will forever stand
For Mr. Longevity, who's known for torching man
When the time is near
I just want you, January, to appear
Tell me your thoughts of our divorce I know
it's unacceptable, of course
May the oceans roar and the skies fall
Forever and ever, it will call
In paradise, may you forever be buried
Forever and ever January

Hidden Paradise

It's within me
Everything . . . My soul, my peace
It's beyond my small and simple dreams
It's buried deep beneath the seams
It's not outside of what I think
But everything that made it shrink
It was the calmness of my storm that made me realize
I don't have to search beyond the twilights or beyond my eyes
To know that the true search of soul lies with me
I'm talking about my paradise, you see
Everything that it is, everything that I need,
and everything that I want is tied to this place . . .
A place where freedom can be free
It's funny; the only thing I really had to see is that paradise was . . . here, beneath the layers of me
Realizing it's not my surrounding environment that gives way to it
Because it'll be that same surrounding environment that takes it away from me
It's my paradise
Hidden away from the world to protect it from the world
To keep me sane in my most insane
The travel time to get there is just a thought
But . . . I just have to think it to know it and be taught
Everything that I am and want to be and the key to unlocking the gate to opening the door . . .
Paradise!

I have to believe in what's in front of me without remorse to what's behind me
To know that paradise exists It's my paradise . . . my hidden paradise . . .
The place where I would take the love of my life,
The place where I would give my final sacrifice,
The place where dreams come to stay,
The place where beauty is its forte
Again it's all in me—not around, not beyond
It starts with that peace that people can't see
The fruit of the world? No.
Money? Not even close.
I can't take any of it to this place
It's definitely not allowed—not even a fragment of a trace
It would only smear the integrity for which it stands
Simply a home for Life's fans

The Portraiture by Mr. Tattered Hands

He prepared the backdrop with true ingenuity and swag
It was trimmed with the finest design he had
He picked a brush and dipped it in a brilliant green
And there with his steadied but tattered hand, he proceeded with his lavish scene
He stroked so effortlessly with creative certainty
As if he had such experience but slow and gentle without urgency My
heart was pounding while he was adjusting me
Even with his brush in his tattered hand, I can tell he was recreating my eyes
His look when they met made a funny throb between my thighs
He captured my innocence and promiscuity all in one
Once he was complete, he smiled and said "Ma'am, I'm done."
He presented to me his latest creation,
Which I loved with great sensation
I thought "What a really artistic and talented man!"
And I asked simply "What happened to your hands?"
He looked down and back up at me with a grateful face
His reply was simple. "I'm blessed to be living among the race."
I gave him a kiss, being a fan. I now understand
Why he painted with such beauty . . . my Mr. Tattered Hands

The Standing Ovation

They see me: successful and motivating
With a gracious heart, I accept
I accept everything that comes along with the acceptation:
criticism and faithfulness
They praise me for what I did
As if their opinions matter that much
The lonely nights they don't see
The triggers of a man apart they'll never know
They will only see their version of me through the perception of how
I give it and not its soul's worth
As I leap forward into continuum,
I would grab for a chance of success and peace
They view me as the puppet master, but I'm only the puppet
They view me in this moment only because it matters
It's the now which has defined me
No past. Just potential for the future.
They see me: successful and motivating
And so I accepted and . . . I took a gracious bow.

The Soul of the Dream Chaser

I reached up, and my soul grabbed forever
My heart has no boundaries
I suffer not from what is.
I starve from what's to come
I chase dreams to the other side of beyond

Rain Dancing

Even though I've experienced my "*Raindrops*" it's in the past
My present is full of brilliant dancers for the cast
We will continue to dance the way ahead as if it's our last
Even though again I've had my share of "*Raindrops*," which forged my sass
Life gives us hope, love, and pain; and I'll keep dancing throughout the rain.
Then once the rain comes again, it'll remind me
I learned the dance in its deluded trance
Life will try again for that's its purpose: to continue the test even 'til I start the strain
And I'll remember what my ancestors have taught me;
My father has preached to me, and my mother prayed for me
To remember to dance in the rain

Double Tethered

I'm my closest friend but worst enemy
I move with weight because I'm a precursor to my own situation
I stand strong because I have to, or I would buckle underneath
walls of doubt that question my every move
I'm tied to the duality of love that has kept me but gave me the
hardest break beyond my threshold
Consuming my abandonment of self-force to evolve into a catalyst . . .
And so here I am . . . tethered from my here and then
Somewhere between my hopeful, good, and natural sin

Hope

It always has been there since the beginning of time for you to realize
Even when you fail and stop believing, it still has our mutual ties
You see, it gets around quite a bit
It encourages others throughout the journey not to quit
Many find it in healing and even in their last hour
It kisses and consoles them as part of its power
It is truly the aspiration of our lives
It moves in us, through us, and for us
It shows through motivation, relationships, love, and faith
It helps us redefine and refine our very purpose
It's not a substance or a rare thing
It floods our lives daily, pouring into our streams
Yes, it is contagious: you have it by just being around someone who's exposed
And modified the condition of ourselves being around it
It perpetuates everything we experience that transpires us
Evolutionizing and revolutionizing us forward
Because it is what it shows It does what it knows
It is the essence of free will that was graced upon us
It supercharges us . . . Enough said . . . well
We all know it and see it. It smiles at us through our smiles,
Through our eyes, through our souls . . .
We can't really put our finger on it.
Even when we're old, it's still there.
It helps us define and refine what we go through (times two)
It is and will always be what I call Hope

And if I . . .

If I had to choose my life over again,
I would change nothing but the receiving of my sins
When I survived, wisdom is what it brought
In my darkest hour, it yielded courageous thoughts
Daring to continue to believe and dream
Refining my perception and its means
And if I could become a perfect saint,
I would make believers out of the ones who say they ain't
I would challenge the small-minded, arrogant scientific thinkers at every turn
I would hit them with "beyond reality" with all they're rhetorical concerns
If I could save the world, I still wouldn't because of God's plan
If I could bring our loved ones back, I wouldn't try and take them from His hands
And if I could change the course of time, I would just let it be
Another ripple in human history
The perception of the existence of the "isms" may they stay . . .
As children, we must wander onto our destined way

Dying to Live

I'm ready to die, to truly live
If I could erase all sin and truly forgive
If I could set my life forward by inspiring my past
I would do whatever it takes to make that last
From the moment it insinuates itself
And everything it correlates with the perspective that enters my mind
Be happy, joyful, understanding without trying
I don't know about you, but I know about me
I'm learning me every day as I define what's in mind to conceive my kind
The kind that walks into life without fear because of how they gave into dying
Waking up one day and saying "Mmm . . . I do feel like flying!"
Not giving in but still letting go to not be a part of this conventional flow
To conceive the mere fact that perception is not always the truth
and the light
But to just be right about everything that is, and what to come in a
reality phase of my mind that's in my mind
I'm dying to live, y'all!
Huh, I want to be more than what I am!
I want to fly high
I want to run fast
I want to be beyond my current past
I'm just dying to live, y'all!
Why can't I? What is living?
Do you think it's just waking up and going from day to day?
Going down at night on my knees to pray
Going through life wishing for things that're not enough?
Or living just another term to describe or discuss?
You tell me I'm dying just to do that!
Am I dying just to wake up and understand and just to be black?
If so, I'm still dying to live; I'm still dying to be more

I mean, am I less now in my current reality?
A Poorer shaping form, begging for everything;
again wishing about everything
I'm just dying to live, y'all!
Opening up my eyes to the new hopeful sunrise
Every new day is a new blessing
Looking at the wealth and everything they have
Looking at the poor (you know, the economy class) I'm dying to live, y'all!
I'm only speaking what's on my mind
If it was so, how can I rewind
And let God take in?
I want to pour into people beyond what I am,
Set generations forward through my hands
I want to live, but what is living? Has it been honestly defined?
Just because you see people sipping on fine wine
Driving around in fancy cars and wearing fancy clothes like life is theirs
I want that same thing because I want life to be mine
I'm dying to live, y'all!
I'm dying to make belief a reality
I'm dying to make dreams come true
Chasing the aftermath of perfect picture Huh,
walking into this sensational view
I'm dying to live to be more
I'm dying to live to set forth
Knowing the beauty and triumph is just a delicate fray
Like a precious newborn hungry for the way
I'm just dying to try
Living life, I'm ready to try to fly!

Hail to the Queen . . . a dedication to Maya Angelou

Hail to the Queen for her literature, arts, and works!
Here comes our Queen for her values and true worth
She was beyond majestic and touched the souls and hearts of everyone she met
She went through life as graceful as a delicate inspiration that felt
An inspiration so strong that it flows through the hearts and minds of giants who will forever change the course of our generation
Stood next to and played on the battlefield of wars of many nations
The essences of her words was profound with time
As we bleed, as we read, she has shown love through it all was divine
Hail to the Queen; she was ravishing in every way
Performing on stage, casting timeless plays from day to day
From a journalist not to someone who was perfect but someone whose thoughts were free
Who cared for something more . . .
She was a Queen of Queens
Many believe that she would live forever
I knew that day would come
She would ascend back up to where she belongs
You see, she was only borrowed from tomorrow . . .
Higher in the essence of greater things
To eternally help pave the way for us to understand happiness and sorrow,
She was and will always be our fair lady.
Hail to the Queen!

33

33 years I've awoken to a new day
33 years I was delivered from harm's way
I've always strived for the upward-bound
Despite my falls, I'm still here—sane and sound
33 years . . . what others may call full "mature" development
The age of The Christ's passing from earthly death to spiritual and supernatural elements
33 . . . said to be the age of my prime
The year spent sifting the blessings that's mine
Sharing thoughts with true friends only
Filling the void of being lonely
Working on creating my ripple
33 attempts, but I just need one to be simple
To reach the masses . . .
The audience speaking when passing
33 years of prayers have always been there
33 years of layers finally peeled
Finally tapped into my inner will

Spiritually Human

Here I am—a spirit experiencing life as humanly as possible
Brought here through human birth in denial of my spiritual connection
This is my true challenge: to be common or to accept my exceptionalism
Ignorance has a way of comforting but undeveloping growth
Sin covers my every thought and position until I understand my spiritual intuition
The key that accesses the toll bridge that cost the meeting of two fairs
In a united form of coexistences, my strength shall be my very fleshly weakness
My spiritual humility shall be the cornerstone to understanding the balance of my connection
You see, it takes the duality of my humanity that centers my spirituality.
Just like I can't experience love without hate . . . that's how it can only be defined
Light shines its best in darkness; so does my spirit in the hollow of my humanly experience
Sometimes I do tread in the water of life
But it's my spirituality that reminds me I'm merely experiencing its strife
And like everything in this experience, like Time promises us all, it will pass
The consistency of the nature of humanity proves nothing lasts
Since the beginning, the depth of the two has been challenged and twain
This false perception exists to bring unrealistic comfort to the brain
Because it's easier to live life without this heavy burden or strain
To deny yourself apart from yourself is starving your core
The balance must exist to build your baseline for your floor

The Chosen Step in My Inevitable Process

I feel alone in my shared journey
With my destination feeling so far
The grooming is at times tedious
Why?
Others are around but not understanding any more than what hey can understand
Humbly, I'm a complex yet simple man
An aid to Life and trying like everyone else to be its biggest contributor
But where I'm at seems thankless and unnoticed I feel like a fool
The leftover of normality that does not excel past expectation
Not feeling like a child of "The Ruler of Many Nations"
I've been loyal as humanly possible
And so now, I struggle but unfailingly here
Telling stories with a vision that exceeds fear
I can't stop now. I'm shaped, fused back together, crystal clear.

In the Gray

Wow . . . How can I make this sound?
By giving you my real-life rhythm and rhyme
To me everything isn't white, black, and so green
Well, what do I mean?
It's in the gray
Life isn't a cookie cutout for us to survive in the white, black, and so green
Things that are out here that hurt and destroy
Things that govern and build our lives which make it stand for something
We don't have to be all or nothing
Sometimes standing in the gray is where we stay
Hmmm . . . I have had a few of those in my life from day to day
It's called the gray.
Because of it, what do you do
When the wrongful thing you're doing is maybe right?
Or when the most rightful thing you're doing is actually wrong,
But it feels like the right thing to do, maybe at the wrong time?
Maybe with the wrong one?
Or maybe just out of sync with God's
plan? But it's all I've learned trying to be a better man
I know what it's like to wrongfully remind
I know what it means; I know how you'll be defined
While the whole time, we try to keep our hearts pure
Even when you're not sure
You have to understand
Like I said, I'm just here . . . trying to stand

In the gray . . .
Because only one person, one human, one man who died and ascended to heaven
The one who truly can shine a light on my past and knows the way
The one who can make sense out of my gray
The one who can assure me it's okay
Many think He didn't stay
But I know He'll always be with me to guide and show me His way
When I look back, I've done all that I could
I mean I know I've done some things I shouldn't have
But I did the best with the love that I was showed
Through it all, I can say
I'm here in the gray

Guarding Love

It was my true and only craft
Fighting Love's wrath
The sun will set on me
Another Love essentially will be

The Tattooed and Pierced Saint

I pray And I lay
They think I'm not like them
Condemned forever in sin
They're so judgmental toward me, and I don't know why
I don't hate them for their hypocritical lies
I pity their misunderstanding of my outer appearance Because I'm tatted and pierced to express my life's experience To them I'm another lost soul in sin
What they don't know is I'm a faithful friend
Because in my eyes, everyone blends
We're all connected in some form of kinship
To them I was the mistake
They are religious in their own traits
Definitely not adhering to the "True Vine"
They continue to look down on and away from me as if I didn't exist What they don't understand . . . I was like them . . . malnourished Partially ingesting the . . . soul food
Being united, not divided, as we are so fooled
Maybe one day, they will see
Beyond their perspective and what's actually ordained to be

Just Passing Through

Walking through
Running through
Looking through
Praying through
Dream chasing through
Either way, I'm passing through
Looking at life through a glass
There I am just walking around, running in and out,
Moving around, and observing everything without a doubt,
Trusting the Man upstairs who will bring me out
I'm just passing through this time through this glass
Wondering how long it'll last
Huh, just passing through . . .
The things that I see
The things that I am
Will not be always
Because I know that through it all
It is not my way
Unpredictable path . . . I'm just passing through
Looking at life through the glass
There I am just walking around in and out,
Observing everything without a doubt,
Trusting the Man upstairs who'll bring me out
I'm just passing through this time, through this glass
Wondering how long it'll last

Walking through
Running through
Looking through
Praying through
Dream chasing through
Either way, we're passing through
How we pass through is indeed up to you

Understanding Love

Love has always had my heart like no other
With majestic wonder that challenges mankind to go further
Who are you really?
Why do you make us do the things we do?
Why are you so hard to understand?
I've watched you literally control man
You are truly life's requirement for the ultimate expression
Unbalancing our version of reality and perception
But I think I've got you figured out; I know how you dance about
Teaching us the rightness of will and choice
Showing us sacrifice and being a sensitive voice
Love, you are very good at what you do
Understanding you would be the truth of truths
As for me learning the truth? I'll take it to my grave
Cause of everything you've done for me and what you gave
It was more than enough, and I'm just keeping it real.
Feelings without the discipline of Love would be truly unfulfilled

Without Wax

I'm broken and torn
In this exterior form
Without wax . . . here . . . sincere
Exposed with all my errors
Humbly broken, staring in a crackly mirror
Refining my core and things that are dear But through it all, I'm here
As long as my heart stays pure,
I will always be prayerfully humble and without wax—sincere

All It Takes is a Dream

The dream in my mind always comes to hand.
Using a pen and paper to tell a tale of different places, different things, and inspirational lands . . .
To me a dream is a path to my purpose
It is eventually a vision that inspires me of greater things.
Beyond what I can see, hear, smell, taste, or touch
The keys to a cage of peer pressure of what I cannot do,
What I try and do; and the key to understanding what successfulness truly is, turned inside out and becomes my reality
Everything that I am that makes me positive in the most valuable way
To inspire others to climb up the ladder toward the best that I can be and beyond
Because without that, what makes it free?
I'm not silly. I know greatness was never free
But I know everything comes with a great cost—something I'm willing to pay to be the boss
Discouragement might come
Sadness will welcome itself; unwanted friends, distrust, and loyalty all might be my next step
But I know I must pass through 'cause I know my dream is bigger than my circumstances
Everything that I am and everything that I want to be are bigger than what surrounds me in this now
It is that vision that inspires me to be more
Because I know all it takes is a dream
A dream that is the purpose and blueprint of what I need to be, where I need to go
It appears in our wind down, unconscious mind-set; but it's planted like a mustard seed in the back of our thoughts

We just have to clear the way of our distractions and see it for what it is
And be humble enough to take the dream, and be faithful rather than fearful to move forward
Because all it takes is a dream to move this way ahead,
to move this way instead of being distracted and discouraged and lying on the roadside
All it takes is a dream to make everything what it needs to be
Oh, you will move and it will cost . . . but that's okay!
Because it's worth it. All it takes is a dream.
To carry yourself to infinity and beyond, all it takes is a dream.
Please don't let me stand in your way from yesterday
Don't let my words contradict what you say
Don't let my dreams stand in your way . . . Be not . . . are you?. . .
I'm not . . . You will always be!
Stand strong because at the end of the day, at the end of your universe, at the centric and fiber in you . . .
All it takes is a dream.
Don't ignore it. Don't be that silly . . . Ha ha!
Because it's just going to haunt you, and it's going to build in your discouragement repertoire
Then you're going to give in to this so-called reality of circumstances that you're living in
Be more than that because "greater is He that is in you than you that's in the world"
Know that, be that because all it takes is a dream that becomes a vision that becomes an action, which is guided purpose.
All it takes is a dream.

Origins of the Poet's Corner

Allow me to tell you of a place where it all comes from
You know, a place where writers and poets bum,
A place where every inspiration is welcome
Here, where Plato teaches and gives advice,
Where Yeats and A. Philip talk about civil rights,
Where Hemingway exchanges thoughts with E.E.
Here, where Edgar shares "spoken words" and thoughts
with Aristotle and Ms. Ruby Dee,
Where Ms. Maya presents a cast
Of a throwback classic play that made us all laugh
It was truly heaven on earth; it was a magical place for
literature birth
It was a palace of mutual and respected thoughts
Sprinkled with a little of entitlement and costs
At the corner of Life and Aspirations, where it laid,
A fantastic structure stood and the source of what was made
At the corner, housed the history of generations
Where Langston and Emily delivered a powerful presentation
Here at the corner, where everything has one voice
Here where creativity was endorsed
Here where they wrote out poems, plays, and lively discussed literature
Here at the cornerstone, where dipped quills forged legendary signatures

The Layers of Me

I'm rooted deep with many foundations
All connected with intertwined and random correlations
But these characteristics are not what define me
Merely my past, present, and possible future family tree
The Soldier
The Barber
The Brother
The Father
The Lover
The Elitist
The Saintliest
The Sinner
The Determined Winner
And still . . . who knows me when I don't know me?
Whose reality? What picture do they see?
What's my measure?
Whose thoughts am I pleasuring?
Despite my many faces tied to thoughts and different places,
They're all still me . . . defined and refined like wine in its process with the help of Time
Through my layers, I learn myself of one too many consolidated minds

Water Proof

I survive life
The water that flows giving it
I am surviving life
Being proof to some things being lifted
It's not about avoiding but absorbing
Growth is the key
I'm among them but not one of them
I'm just passing through
Turning hearts, meshing understanding, revealing one truth
Being proof, surviving life . . . I am waterproof !

Nite Lyfe

It was enjoyable like a fix
An admirable Nite of excitement Venturous as a great hunt
Drawn by attraction of this enticing mix
The scent of a thousand women's personalities
Intoxicated by the effects of sexual intent
Edging it all with a mood-filled mint
Tasting it all in this fanatical, surreal reality

The hunger of being on the scene
The streets are lit up and full
Crowds are everywhere being so erotically cruel
It's like the most addictive fiend

Was it the laughter that made the Nite wild?
Was it the flirting or the finest woman that looked and smile?
Either way, I take it all in

Absorbing it as a proud and delightful sin
There's nothing more sweeter than this fling of the Nite
This enticing portrait of Lyfe
Tasting the different flavors of nectar of the Nite
Viewing the different intense shades hosted by Lyfe

Defining Atlas

Throughout time, *we* carry and endure the changing world
All of its joy, happiness, sorrow, and pain
We hunger for the temptations of Life; the thought of dying to Life scares *us*
A Titan in *our* own standards . . . *We* are defining and refining *our* purpose
Every day living another day that God has made while learning the secrets of Life
We stand again as if *our* destiny was meant to be
Here I am. Judge me if you may
Gracefully and strategically, I navigate through it all
Or along with *others*, do *we* plan our inevitable fall, which I feel *we* must do without a doubt?
If not, how can God come in and bring *us* out?
The story of my perspective of man is all I want to tell
Its journey to and from with its touch of Heaven and Hell
I'm trying and trying to make people understand
Telling a story without a script and director—just this pen
I visualize it all in just one fade
Over and over again . . . you know, same story with different shades
But inevitably, it's all for *us* to grow
Atlas is simply a symbol of *our* longtime history
The truth to *our* parallel mystery
A beacon of strength and endurance
To remind us all of *our* sacrificial assurance

More

I've always wanted to be *more* than I am
Why can't I be *more* ? . . . It's a type of longing to reach your ultimate potential . . . if such an extensive limitation like one exists
We cry, stress, and act out daily wondering the hows and whys of this catered abyss
We do it to get *more* than we have until we get it and want *more*
When does it become greed? You know . . . *more* than just faithful deeds . . .
It's a timeless obsession through man's extensive journey through this world and beyond.
When do humbleness and truth step in and guide us to our core spiritual home? Back to our source that paid our big loan?
More is not good or evil but a tool, and like most things, we have to understand the directions to see its true affections.
One, I must say, that can deceive us from our flawless, divine imperfections

I, Wonderer

Have you ever wondered more?
It's burning deep inside to the outside
So curious about beyond
What is the circle of "just of"?
What lies behind the curtains?
I want to see
Mystifying mystique
But I can't . . . it's not my time
I'll just have to wait 'til the moment is refined

Standing on the Edge of . . . the Breaking/ the Awakening

Well, it's here and so am I!
The socalled catalyst crossroad of my life
It would be here that everything would come into focus
I try to deny it or turn away from it
Because I didn't understand it
I'm leaning forward, not back because I'm not afraid anymore
To lose for the gain
I'm not afraid of the requirement of sacrifice because I believe
For I have grown through my long and tedious transition
Knowing the He is the key to my *man* . . .
And I accept, and so I leap into my whatever-life-brings welcomed existence
And here I stand on the edge
Of not knowing tomorrow's pledge
But do know what I can forge instead Awakening . . .
challenged by the daily bread

Lost Love Found

It was the very commitment tied to its emotional duality, and it was made perfect
In everything it is and does,
From its selfless essences,
It will take you over and beyond you
It will find you in your abyss and superficial senses
And its potentially poisonous kiss can ruin or enhance lives
But without it, mankind would only be defined through its own secured lies

Not Chained

No longer chained by your conception of me
Freed beyond measure and realization of the "just be"
What's wrong? I'm not the color of your shade
I live now beyond the formerly known facade
You will only know me now as I was
Without apprehension of who and what I love
Changed but not chained
Estranged but now gained
Again, my path forward
My all . . . not chained . . . moving onward

The Dark Path to Light

Sometimes I wonder my circumstances and my embrace
Of Heaven's and Hell's face
Even though it feels like it; I am not alone even here I try
not but 'cause of Adam's curse, I do have fear
But I'm strong, or I would not be on this path
Yes, invitation only to push through the aftermath
Despite its difficulty, I'll still find my way
With He who shines . . . to be the completest, I must stay

The Tears that Flow So-Lo

Pain has finally found me
If I never see the rise of tomorrow,
May the grace from yesterday may I please borrow?
Only if Time permits, may I, sir, vent?
As the displacement of my
Psychological, biological, physiological, unconditional condition checks in
To evaluate my sins
It was all a press
Just to let the tears flow solo to make such a mess
But I'm here to deliver the rest
I'm here standing by my best

Even though the tears flow so-lo,
They will stop
My life will move forward with its growth
And clean up every drop

The Kaleidoscope

Among everything we do, yes, we collide
But there is something more than hope
Is it the beautiful black and white
That makes everything easier to decide wrong from right?
Or is it that beautiful gray that justifies all our sins?
Could it be the blind ignorance and stubbornness that won't let us give in?
It's as beautiful and innocent as a baby trying to figure it out
What to think, what we know, and why we really pout
But then again, we all beautifully collide
Merging our many forms into one facade
Because all we see is this and that through our tubes
Which we all abuse
In this, we were conceived in our rawest nature; but it's still a design
Running our mouths by what's really yours or mine
Does it matter? Because of our spiritual or developmental state
Or just simply knowing that you are a part of the bigger beautiful collide . . .

Evolving

Growth is undeniable
Change is always
Being the better of me is imminent
Knowing myself is instinctively to be
I am becoming simply . . .
The challenge is always there
So is my strength ready to bear

Elatedly Elevated

I feel something that's so great
It pumps through my heart like a pounding ape
It's because I finally know me. "Hi, Me!"
I know my position and can finally breathe
The air is so cooled and fresh up here
In the place where I relax and not have fear
Backlashes to my actions down below
But it's okay though
You see, I've been there . . . in the bottomless pit of hopeless and no
That's where I was made in my process and broken in my sew
Then I had to understand the breach and reach of what I owe
The wage was more than enough
But the betrayal and the struggle upward-bound was beyond tough
And so the process purges for the greatly cost
The Potter shaping was undoubtedly skimming, every little lost
And at every level, it happened over and over again
I smiled when I didn't and I tucked my chin
I supported when I felt anger (and wanted revenge)
I showed up when I wanted to walk away and gave beyond everything
And I stayed beyond my welcome and still paid
And through it all . . . this step is high
But now I'm no longer bound by its try
Of intimidation and wasted manipulation
I see beyond current situations
I smile now because I'm elated
I support now because it's all related
I show up now because I don't have to walk away
And I stay now because I understand He's already paid

Legacy

Here it is . . . what I live to be Hope
and dreams beyond just me Cured of
death's hand
Striking to stand
Leaving the residue of the aged anew
If tomorrow would ever fold
This will always be told
Not myth but the renderings of truth
The echoes of timeless cues
For this moment is identified as a lifetime
Streamlining my works of the daily grind
The struggle that defines the overcome
Forever Life's pupil, leaving lessons for future generations to learn

I'll Carry

I'll defend
I'll help mend
I'll pour
I'll restore
I'll be here
I'll try and be near
I'll lend you my heart
I'll reach so we want be apart
I'll give it all because I can
As much as a man
And still here I am
Flawed in every manner
And here . . . to carry

The Moonlight that Shines on my Shadow

Its shine exposes the darkest side of me
Tied up iniquity trying not to be consumed of this world
Only drawn to its light, I see my wrongs converted right
Shining like a star, I wish for divine intuition
Moving forward with dedicated persistence
And like my shadow's purpose of being behind me,
So shall my past and its cast
The ones that didn't make it through my filter of my better me and my season
So the next time the moon shines on my shadow, it'll remember the reason
My prayer, the urge to care, burdens that bare,
But most importantly . . . the graceful fare

Power

It's the balance between whose version is winning or losing
It continues to tip the scale of weak and strong
Cloaked behind history's greatest efforts, it was there
Standing and waiting to be used and sometimes abused
It showed us love and equally hate
It showed prosperity while planning for treachery
It thrives for submission but prays for challenges
Its firm hand but soft heart lie with who holds it without reservation
But capable of destroying lives while securing others
Some believe it affects the just and unjust alike without boundaries
When guided, it motivates
But it's never to own but merely to borrow
In the instant and perilous world we live in,
I constantly pray for the hope and righteousness of tomorrow

Residue

Life is hard when you have residue
Cleaning out your Life's closet when you know what you've been through
I'm not in charge like I thought I would be
Now, I understand there are bigger things than selfish me
I'm living now with a humble bleed
Mercy has come to intercede

I Find Anew

Hope was always mine
It sprang from my heart like a precious vine
It kept me sane in all of this Anew
When my life was changing from what I knew
Love kept me from being a monster in my chaotic storm
It allowed for me to keep compassion, to be stronger than the norm
It helped to truly understand the purpose of this cause
Joy kept me committed and my belief in the Anew
Knowing it's the primary ingredient in why I grew
It showed me the invaluable worth of living from day to day
And how not to be and move ugly things out the way
I find a new . . . type of patience I find a new . . . deeper morality
My purpose is becoming clearer and true
I . . . find . . . Anew

Blaque Reign

Beautiful, I thought she was
More than extravagant in every way
So many words I just can't say
Just to fall in her steps is indeed a privilege
Dangerous and seductive she was
The deadliest combinations of addiction
Irresistible in the most lustful desires
Poison will kill, so be it
Oh, Ms. Reign, come kiss me
Draw me in your sexual hunger
Wrap me around your finger
Heal me of my great depressions of life
I will do anything to have another hit
Come, oh beautiful Blaque Reign.
Let's escape this world!
Come, entangle me in the highest of highs
My mind and soul are yours
Attractions are the concept that binds us
I feel you all through my body
Making my heart pump faster and faster
Many people try to stop us from being together
I can't stop
Who cares about the consequences of our love?
Life is about finding the thing your soul desires
Who cares if you're an illusion?
You're my illusion!

My So-Called Reality

Sometimes I feel the world spins around me one hundred miles per hour
Like I'm on a merry-go-world that won't stop
I know I can't quit life
So I can't jump off the merry-go-world
All I can do is admire the spin,
Take note of the sins,
Treasure the moments,
Be mindful of the wants,
Speak and pray for the despair
And genuinely care,
Offer my heart
And let Love dissect it apart,
Be true beyond perception
And don't live with its ugly cousin, deception
Understand karma,
Love momma, Respect dad,
Because for me, he gave me all he had.
Pour into others what I can,
And take my beautiful girl's hand
Try not to fast-forward through it all
Because it's important that I see my falls
Always remember Him, who judged us but didn't pass

The one, who no matter what, didn't treat you and I like an outcast
Watching daddy's princess become a queen
Her being God's gift to a man's dream
Understanding my son and making him become a better man
Watching him become a foundation, building a home that can stand
But I guess that's everything . . . watching my life on this merry go world
Watching me and everything that could be
It's all good here . . . any day above ground, I always say
Taking it in day by day
They say it's just *reality* and maybe so . . . or just how I show my glimpse of reality and growth

I Know

I know why you fear me
I know why you watch me
Because I have my father's eyes
Being created in His image was no surprise
I know your secret
It's been underlined the whole time
It's been in things, emotions, and even in love, destruction, and lies
I know why I bother you
Because I represent the better greatness of you
I'm flawed but I'm still perfect
I'm wrong but still correct
I finally got it figured out!
I know why you look down on me
A slave with a future moving about
A slave with hopes and dreams and without doubts
You see, I know that nations are lifted through my stride
I know my hands represent the struggle of times
I know my progress is catastrophic
I know I'm filled with well-deserved pride I know my roots
I know my ancestors
I know why God smiles when he looks at me
I know who believes
And I'm here because of that growth
Ignorance is no longer my excuse Finally . . . I know

Freedom

Caught in a fight
Can't go on; Hope is present.
Lord, give me the might,
Strength has been sent.
Serving the oppressed
With a slaved mind, we function.
Imprisoned, we all are blessed
This is some cursed, freewill assumption.
Through life we live; through life we experience
Experiences of sensations
Beyond the senses and minds of reality
Yes, reality gets in the way of dreams
The mental freedom that we all need
Doing our own thing the body bleeds
Due to the conception of this reality
Full of they-say and strives we make
Toward effort to deal with such a thing
But die trying to make this reality my freedom
Only through death we are free; then, we can enjoy freedom.
"Freedom is a gift of free will. Beyond this reality, does it truly exist? What's in the beginning shall set the stage for true impressions, and through the end, you will know the purpose of the beginning."

Spring Love

Of course, it was here; and the grass was greener than green
Happiness, laughter, and joy was all around; this always happens around spring
It was truly an aphrodisiac for all who can admit it
And then I saw her . . . She was truly a beautiful spirit!
She was as admirable as a precious gem glistening in the sun
Man, how she made my heart burn!
I saw her. Where? I don't know But I'll never forget her glow
I thought I went to heaven, but there she was
Here . . . just walking around without an escort . . . an angel that escaped from above
Love was instant, and I felt so . . . unplugged
She was there, and her eyes made my heart throb
I do consider it robbed
I don't know what it is about the spring
Maybe we do bloom like flowers and show our tempting addictions like fiends
It's all precious and beautiful because we know we're temporary
The mood in the air made me merry
I had it bad.
She was looking, smiling. I never felt so glad
I approached her like an ol' flame
With so much confidence in my game
Made her blush from ear to ear
She entertained
She knew and I knew that there was a part two to what we wanted to do

So I left my name and number, and hopefully she'll think of me
Mmm . . . we'll see!
Maybe I'm just being lame.
I never believed in love at first sight . . . nothing but pain
But it wasn't even a sight—a glance, I must say
But 'til this day, I'll give anything and everything . . .
It was love.
She knew what it was
So I check in with her to see . . .
God knows what He's doing for my belief
The world seemed more beautiful after being in her space.
She was as admirable as a precious gem glistening in the sun
Man, she made my heart burn!
She had my heart all over the place
She was the essence of what Heaven would be in human form
She was only here for the spring, and then she was gone
We ran, we played, we kissed
She will always be remembered . . . as refreshing as morning mist
Spring love . . . Bliss!

The Night . . . I Had Me

The Night I was low, she was there listening
She was there consoling
I told her of my problems, and she reminded me how good life was
She was beautiful in every way
I was hoping she would stay
For a while, you know, and keep me company
As I sit with her, the Night, she's not scary or creepy
Not all those things we make her out to be
I welcomed her into my liberty
The Night is definitely my companion through my journey
She kept me sane and provided a lot of clarity and understanding
As we move forward, I prayed and hoped that she'll never forsake me
As I continue to view Life through my kaleidoscope,
My purpose was refined with her, my Night
It was my date for destiny that was beyond my sight
How can something so beautiful be born not of light but
continue to shine so bright?
In her profound words that she shared,
She reassured me someone always cares

The Runaway

I run into loneliness
I run away from being meshed, pressed,
Away from the norm of what society rules as best
So I run to fulfill my quest
And then I'll take a knee, pray, be thankful, and finally rest
So 'til then, I'll run
And run fighting through, not fitting
Even belittling
I'll run to fulfill my quest
And then I'll take a knee, pray, be thankful, and finally rest.

The Sweet Ode to Meymaneh

Here's to everything for which we cared
To the hot days and cool nights we shared
To the adventures as Soldiers that nearly cost
To the tragedies we lost
To the winters that I'll never forget
To the horrible heat waves that made me regret
To the people who should
For the nation that could
To our number one fans
To the one who helped us stay united to stand
We were heroes for the time
Hopefully making a difference with our lives on the line
She was a beautiful hunting place
In our hearts is now where she stays
Looking back at her from across the oceans far from a distance
Her secret is safe . . . her commitment will always be a remembrance
She was home to the fallen and refuge for the fighters
We protected her well with volleys
To the team, we'll always care
To found memories we share
In the desert, she will always lay
To the sweetness of her days
May the souls there rest in peace
A salute, a flag lowered, and honor for her belief

Limited

I'm new, but I'm old
Not limited beyond my means and methods
But limited because I'm special
Special beyond the heavens and everything that surrounds me
That I'm among . . . limited
In the very sight of that, in an instant, I'm gone
I am so rare and the rarest of all breeds;
I'm just merely passing through this world
From what it supersedes
Caring and baring everything that comes with this world
I'm limited . . . not necessarily to limitation
But I'm limited
I will not be here always
Impressions of my time here will always be set forth here
History is what we're creating, what I'm living
Yeah, I'm limited
Limited edition . . . Limited in rarity
Because I am and will always be
But not always here
The very best thing that could
Ha! Yeah, I'm limited. Isn't it funny?
We are rare . . . in the rarest form
I am limited. Isn't it crazy? I'm a limited edition
Passing through . . . through and through this world

I have an expiration date . . . yeah, that makes me limited
But it's okay because things that are limited become a collector's item
And who's the collector?
Mmm . . . Some argue but nevertheless We have to
I'm limited . . . aren't you?

The Juggernaut

Struggle and pain . . . That's everything that I am
Empower me with thy grace and mercy
Strength and service in my heart . . .
These are what you charged me
The undeniable force that lurks beneath in the core of our hearts
It draws and pulls on us like a relentless bad habit
I use it . . . Misguided, it could be dangerous
There I go trying to be
There I go just wondering . . . Me? Is this what I'm about?
I feel that strength . . . my juggernaut
It's difficult to explain
But it remains the same
The hunger of something better
The drive to go to the beyond
The pursuit and the will of a flawed victor
Knowing what I am not . . .
Curious about what I could be
Here . . . ready . . .
My Juggernaut!

Sweat on the Rifle

I was a soldier once—not young but still I am
The blood we shared, the lives we spared
They say it's for liberty, but sometimes it becomes a gray area.
We're in harm's way protecting them from their own selves and enemies.
The crosses we carry
The salute that we gave
For a fallen comrade whom we praised
The bowed head at the graves
It was protected, guarded—America's gate.
It was the night, the summertime, the heat, and the late.
One thing I can say: it was us that stood at the gate.
Sweat, tears, blood, and lives . . . We shared the ache.
Everything that pumps brother and sisters in arms, I say
Many come home in a wooden box, in a casket.
They'll be remembered by immortality through time.
I counted down the days when war would be over, and days will be back mine
I thought I was going to be marked off.
You know the list—the list of opportunities
The father, husband, brother, sister, or mother
Who knows when the next one will be?
We locked and loaded our weapons and ran many missions
From Iraq to Afghanistan to Kuwait . . . Democracy and constitution
Everything for our country we were willing to lay
Down and fight or protect nations who were too weak to defend themselves

Tears pouring down on tainted dog tags
Tears coming down on the bloody dirt, staining the sand
It flows like a river on these foreign lands.
They say we're messed up, you know.
I lay it down the same. The chess games we play
Sweat on the rifle is what saved the day.
The power of God is with you, but whose side is He on?
It's like moving chess pieces on a board
The victory is already won.
If we could just make peace out of all this madness I don't know . . .
We said all over again "Why can't we just all get along?"
Let bygones be bygones. We're all just human beings.
In the end . . . all of this chips at the soul of a man
Killing another man for a cause we think is so much bigger
Only when we get to the end do we all realize we're all just used.
A tool maybe but we all have roles to play
Mine was the soldier (so proud). I carried the flag on my arm
Old faithful . . . The star spangled banner . . . Sweat on the rifle . . . kept everything in order
To my brother and sisters in arms across the world
I must say this: for the cause that was great,
I say I served with real heroes.
Hopefully I'll see you again. RIP.
We guarded her gates for the country that could, for the people who should.

Marking it Forward

Only when I'm dead and gone will I leave my mark
When I leave this world is when it will start
I see the world differently, but I don't know why
It's like I see it with everyone else but with different eyes
Same tears and smiles but different reasons for cries
Understanding the reasons for all the tries
Only when I'm dead and gone will I leave my mark
When I leave this world is when it'll start
How torturous it is to move throughout history!
Without purpose of what's failure and victory
Now I'm here standing upright, and my vision has never been so clear
Refining myself toward the mark now for the first time . . . without fear

Losing to Win

You see it's not about me for it to be for me
I must understand that to lose to myself is to win for the better of myself
Learning to give beyond what's left,
Learning how not just to be
It is unacceptable in the humanly character of me
To just be
It's "going against the grain" to simply not apply
To not ask those wondering questions of "why"
But sometimes, those are just selfish and misguided ambitions
Design and meant to build on false pretension
And so-called intuitions
And here I am . . . renouncing self
And here I am . . . understanding the true victory of press
But just to know that losing to self is to win at God's best
And that is our deepest test

Untitled (Repentance)

Covered in the darkness of my soul
Plunging into this deep sea of eternal cold
Receiving what I thought was
the upper hand But it was only my quicksand
Using redemption as a sense of forgiveness
But catering to sin as it belongs
Stretching my hand too strong
To what we know . . . Truthfulness

Black Paper

Before there was white, it was me—like darkness to light
The foundation
I was the darkest form of usage
I am the shamed past, underrated present, and no good future
Understanding that I was created to enhance civilization
But feared to be an abomination
Like the grimiest gear in the clock that leverages the time and date
And still I'm here . . . black as the ink that writes our fate

In-Lighting

It separates our good and bad . . . our darkest secrets
Defines us from our would be self-imposed enemies
Binding us through our consciousness we call *guilt*
Beyond our stupors, it helps mold our core character
Without it . . . we would fall into the denial of self and suicide
to our inner fuse
Then abuse will become the only detrimental escape
But I always thank God for the latter
For the strength and will it takes
Shines so bright
Shines so right
Originally based . . . that light

The Deaf Messenger

I never heard a sound
Passing through Life's corridor
Viewing only but trying to speak to understanding
Muted only to pass a message through the Body
A sound is not as important as what caused it
And my sound will be the last message for the Body

Feeling Different to Feel the Difference

Consciousness holds the repository of resilience seen only through a blind eye
In its worst moments, it pushes us to live or die
And then under the umbrella of practicality and logic, we ask . . . why.
When our perspective changes, the difference can become a lie
And so we are left feeling different, but we must know the difference
It's always our move or choice; feeling the difference is just our internal voice,
The beacon that guides and drives us through our humanly spiritual war

The Blood's Key

Truly the charge that paid the way throughout time
Shattering so-called societies' moral compasses
It tied and broke families and created new ties
It brought salvation
And waged civil wars
Blood has always shifted man's appetite
It held the binding thread of Life and Death
It's what God had left
It's the footing of survival kept

The Fall

Why do we fall so close and dear,
Believing the same belief is not so near,
Treading in trending waters,
Thinking we're coasting different charters?
Fools, we are . . . thinking our trip is fueled of our own esteem!
Only when it ends do we realize it wasn't what it seems
We all fall the same but in different manners
How we get up is the difference in our successful banners
The meaning of it all is inevitable we do and must fall
It's the epic climax of our God-given cause
And so we embrace with a faithful case
We are charged with a do-diligent heart
It's as innocent as a tear from a baby
The humility of not knowing the way up . . . pure . . . hazy

The Memorial . . . The Funeral . . . The Outro

We had a party today like no other
We celebrated a homecoming of a dear
mother She was a true inspiration to us all
Tears of joy for someone who lived for a greater cause
We reminisced about her life at glance
We gave many praises and danced
We sang music from our hearts
Wishing her well as she departs
We all gathered and told our version of the story
And how at her party she looked so glorious
She was looking her stunning best
For her exiting the bittersweet stage of life to retire and rest
We'll miss her so much even though it'll only be for a while
You are forever in my heart, and I will never forget your smile.
Next time the wind blows, I will stop and take the extra breath
Knowing that it came from you, wishing us all blessed
And lastly, when the sun leaves its beautiful mural across the skies,
I'll know truly you're in paradise!

Scent of a Woman

Her aroma was enticing and tantalizing
She smelled liked the sweetest perfume and natural oils.
Her smell . . . well, you know . . .
It turns the hearts of hearts, making every man mush
She was intoxicating in every way
She could have her way
I smell her all the way from across the room
It grabbed my heart and masculinity
It drew me in like bait Maybe it was just fate
The image of well-mixed perfumes in a fine crystal glass
She knew what she was doing
It was the scent of woman . . . intoxicating and desirable . . .
Sexually touching the basis of my sensual core, making it rise . . .
what it really means to be Eve
But she was also everything that came with Eve's Deception;
innocent at heart, misguided . . . yes
Before . . . She was us; she was all that and then some
I could not reject her, watching her nice backside . . . that's what I
wanted to do . . .
She pursued with a strategic purpose
She drew it in . . . Losing was not an option for her
The scent was there
Yeah, dangerous she was and mysterious in every way
I knew all of these things, and I still played
That scent was the emancipation of all fine women—maybe
womankind in general

It was rare, but it was there; I knew it and she did too
Watch out! This ain't about the blues: it's about a clue.
A woman... tantalizing and seductive in every way Yeah, and I still chose to play
But she couldn't stop
Man, I smelled her blocks and blocks and miles and miles!
I knew when she was around, and I knew when she left.
Mmm ... the scent of a woman ... Without them, what would be left?
It is ... irresistible.
The scent ... wow ... that was some good ...
Mmmm ... the scent

Hero

From one thousand words, maybe I protect
Created from the foundation of my father's love that commands respect
From one thousand eyes, maybe I disguise
You know . . . love one's most intimate deceitfulness and lies
It's hard; it's difficult, but that doesn't mean it's impossible
I know I don't wear a cape or a utility belt or have special powers beyond what the eye can see
But I'm here with everything: freedom of the mind and soul.
Watching and waiting, making sure everything is . . .
You see, a hero is not one who flies around in an iron suit.
Or maybe it's just someone that you see every day that looks like us but keeps us, protect us, loves us,
At the root, Mom, Dad, Uncle, Aunt, Brother, and Sister—they may all be
Because they're here for you and me
Maybe a stranger or maybe your next-door neighbor
With a good heart and positive motivation, they can tell their own story
How they did something heroic, and they didn't even know it was that
Until someone mentioned their heroism back
So I thank you a thousand times for who and wherever you may be
For the one who volunteered to share the unconditional burden with me
Up, up, and away I go
From zero to hero again . . . mmm . . . I go

P.S. To You

Well, I've done what was needed
In my epic cause,
I tried to reshape and redefine without a pause
Everything I have done should hang in the hall
The Hall of Immortals, I hope,
Where Love will pass through to see
Sadness may stop through to loaf
Maybe Joy will come just to be among friends who believe
Then Heartache will try and watch from a distance
It really tries to be consistent
Time will come by and pay its respect
Knowing it's not a threat
And of course, Victory will show up to prove it won the bet
Well, I've done what was needed
In my epic cause,
I tried to reshape and redefine without a pause
Everything I have done should hang in the hall
The only one I prepare to show among them all
The one I want to see before the curtain falls
The one who will grace us with its wisdom and faith in this place
The great teacher who pours into me and you
It's here . . . Welcome, Life! Thank you for being true

It wrote a meaningful note to inform us of the long-waited purposes that
we played toward the hall . . .
Cheers to everyone who helped plan this magnificent ball!
Before Life left, it gave me a personal card that said
"To my dearest friend, thanks for participating and holding on all the way
through.
P.S. This was never for me, but it was always for you."